SCOTTISH MOTOR TRACTION CO. LTD.

AN ALBUM OF PHOTOGRAPHS

by

D. L. G. HUNTER, C.Eng.

1978

TURNTABLE PUBLICATIONS

SHEFFIELD

OTHER BUS TITLES:

Scottish Buses Before 1928
Edinburgh Corporation Bus Album
The "Western" Story, Parts 1 & 2
First Bus in West Yorkshire
Buses in Leeds
MacBraynes for the Highlands

First Published 1978

© DLG Hunter, 1978

ISBN O 902844 46 6

PRINTED IN GREAT BRITAIN

by

Henry Boot Group Printing

INTRODUCTION

"SMT" — the term is still often used for Eastern Scottish Buses — was one of the largest and best known bus companies fifty and more years ago, although for some time after its founding, in June 1905, it was always referred to by its full title "Scottish Motor Traction". The company was set up to serve the countryside around the City of Edinburgh, and having drawn up a rigorous specification, and examined several vehicles, a public service commenced between Edinburgh and Corstorphine on New Years Day 1906 with the first of five Maudslay 34-seat double-deckers. Other Maudslays followed quickly and later four Rykneilds, some of each make being charabancs. The livery was green and cream. The company and its operations, ably guided by W. J. Thomson, were a success from the start and routes expanded steadily to include Queensferry, Uphall, Penicuik, Loanhead, Rosewell and Gorebridge, as well as day tours further afield in summer.

The management wanted a much better bus, however, and proceeded to design and build its own 32-seat saloon, employing the Minerva Silent-Knight engine. The first of them appeared in 1913, appropriately christened the "Lothian" and about 100 were built, including some for other operators, up to 1924, when production ceased. The design was far ahead of any of its contemporaries. The company also engaged in a large trade in the supply and repair of motor vehicles of all kinds, and sold and hired Lothians.

Two Albion charabancs augmented the fleet just before the First World War, but were commandeered by the army. Lothians continued to be built, however, some being provided with charabanc bodies and by the end of the war, although the old Maudslays and Rykneilds had now gone, the fleet numbered about fifty. During the latter part of the war all the Lothians were provided with gas-bags so that services could be kept running though petrol was very scarce. A handful of old vehicles acquired at this period from firms which had succumbed did not last long.

After the war the network of routes was considerably expanded to serve Linlithgow, Bathgate, Whitburn, Balerno, Ormiston and Haddington. Local routes were run in West Lothian and in 1920 a base was set up in Dundee from where services started to Blairgowrie, Forfar, Arbroath, etc.

A large number of Thornycrofts, both buses and charabancs, was bought, followed by 14-seat Fiats for some of the longer routes and tours. The Fiat charabancs were painted brown whereas other charabancs were pale yellow. A few vehicles wore a grey livery for a year or two at this period. The Thornycroft buses had S.M.T. bodies and some were forward-control models. All the Lothians and many of the Thornycrofts were fitted with pneumatic tyres in the early twenties. The Lothians outlasted all the others, many being still in service in 1930. By the mid-twenties more-modern buses could be obtained from various makers and for further expansion the company ordered a large number of Maudslays and Albions. Except for coaches and a few of the Albions these were forward-control models, with full-front cabs as favoured by the company. There were also a few small Beardmores and Internationals, which did not last long.

The company bought out a number of small operators at this time and also the Galashiels firm of Brook & Amos, which owned some fifty vehicles, bringing the S.M.T. total to about 400 in 1926. Routes now extended to Boness, Glasgow, West Calder, Peebles, North Berwick and throughout the Border counties. The next two or three years saw more acquisitions and long distance routes as far as Newcastle and Carlisle. In 1928 Star buses and coaches replaced some of the Fiats and 1929 saw orders for Leylands, including "Titans", the first double-deckers since the original Maudslays of 1906. The company continued to flourish, still under W. J. Thomson, and in 1929 was reconstituted with railway investment and a controlling interest in other large Scottish bus companies of more recent origin.

Long-distance routes to Inverness, Dumfries, Blackpool, Liverpool, Manchester and London commenced in 1930. Also in 1930 there was a change of livery to blue for all vehicles, though over the next few years there were several variations in styling and a number of coaches carried a dark navy blue livery, while cream reappeared for some others in 1937. A fleet numbering scheme was introduced in 1931 covering nearly 500 vehicles; hitherto the Edinburgh or Dundee licence numbers had been used, or local fleet numbers for the Borders and at Bathgate. Large numbers of A.E.C.'s, Bedfords, and Leylands were bought over the next nine years. The first diesel bus, an A.E.C., appeared in 1931 and from 1933 all new vehicles except the Bedfords had oil engines. The Bedfords were of several sizes, including some 12-seaters suitable for the narrow roads in the north-west Highlands.

In 1940 the fleet totalled about 700 vehicles and releases to the company during the war included sixty utility Bedfords, several Guy double-deckers and a few Dennis single-deckers. Several A.E.C. and Leyland coaches, released from long distance routes now suspended, were provided with more useful double-deck bodies. Following the Second World War the company concentrated on A.E.C.'s and Bedfords and also rebodied many of the older buses. New coaches were now painted cream and in 1949 green was re-adopted for buses. Again there were some variations in styling.

The company's bus and coach department, including its subsidiary operating concerns, was acquired by the British Transport Commission as from 1 April 1948 and registered as Scottish Omnibuses Limited, though it was agreed the fleet name "SMT" would continue to be used for a time. Some rationalisation of services followed, the SMT routes around Dundee being transferred to Alexanders in 1950. Otherwise there was little apparent change, but Bristol coaches appeared in 1954, followed by "Lodekkas" in 1956 and some Leyland PD2/20s in 1957. There were also a few Guys from London, some of which were rebuilt with single-deck bodies, two Albions and the company's own experimental lightweight bus, only one of which was built, in 1955.

Thereafter the SMT fleet name gradually gave way to Scottish Omnibuses and later Eastern Scottish, so a Scottish Motor Traction album ends at this point. The large number of small firms acquired over the years brought into the fleet a correspondingly varied and interesting collection of vehicles of so many different types that a book twice the size of this one would be required were they to be included. We therefore illustrate only the vehicles bought new by the Scottish Motor Traction Company. A comprehensive history and fleet list can be found in the Author's "Edinburgh's Transport", published by the Advertiser Press Ltd., Huddersfield.

1. The first double-deck Maudslay, S543, when six years old. (Travel Press & Publicity Co. Ltd.)

2. A Maudslay with Thomson's radiator and new Stagg & Robson body in 1911.

3. One of the second lot of Maudslays with wider body and transverse seats.

4. One of the Maudslays with charabanc body.

5. Albion charabanc of 1914.

6. The first Lothian 32-seat saloon bus.

7. The standard pattern of Lothian bus.

8. A Lothian bus running on town's gas.
(Travel Press & Publicity Co. Ltd.)

9. Lothian charabancs as later running on pneumatic tyres.

10. A group of 14-seat Fiat charabancs.

11. A Thornycroft charabanc: there were several different body styles.

12. A Thornycroft bus in the grey livery.

13. Thornycroft forward-control 32-seat bus.

14. The first of the S.M.T.'s new 32-seat saloons in 1926 were Maudslays, ten with S.M.T. bodies, 25 with Short Bros. bodies and 25 with bodies by Vickers, of which this is one, later numbered K132.
(Travel Press & Publicity Co. Ltd.)

15. There were also Maudslay coaches with bodies by Short Bros. and by Hoyal. One of the latter is shown, later K18.

16. One of a small number of 28/29-seat Albion saloons which arrived in 1926-7. Later A75.

17. Two Albions were 32-seat saloons with half-cabs. These were later numbered A43-4.

18. A large number of Albions followed in 1927 with 29-seat full-front bodies. This one was later A58. Note the special headboard for the Glasgow Limited Stop service.

19. There were still many more Maudslays such as this one of 1929 with S.M.T. 32-seat body, later K59.

20. Replacing the small Fiat charabancs were Star coaches with 14-seat bodies by Short Bros. This one was later N4.

21. The small buses were also replaced with 20-seat Star saloons. The bodies by Hall-Lewis and by Hoyal were similar. This one was later N37.

22. Later some of the Star buses received 18-seat coach bodies by Alexander Motors, Edinburgh. This one was N35.

23. Double-deckers reappeared in 1929 in the form of the Leyland Titan. A second lot has enclosed stairs. One of the first lot is shown: it was later J22.

24. One of the many 31-seat Leyland Lions of 1929. Later G11.

25. There were also Leyland "Tiger" coaches in 1929 with 29-seat bodies by Cowieson. This one was later H17.

26. In 1937-8 most of these received new 35-seat bus bodies. H29 is shown.

27. Leyland "Tigers" with 26-seat Burlingham bodies were provided for the long distance coach services in 1930. The one shown was later H46.

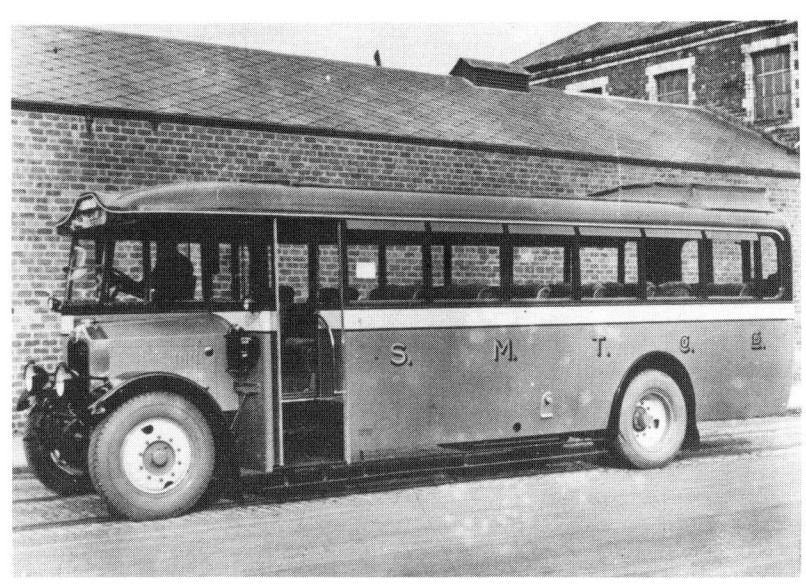

28. Three Albion "Valkyries" with 32-seat Cowieson bodies arrived in 1931. They were A96-8.

29. The 1931 coaches were A.E.C. "Regals" with 28-seat Cowieson bodies. B10 is shown.

30. The first oil engine bus was also an A.E.C. with 30-seat Strachan body, numbered B2.

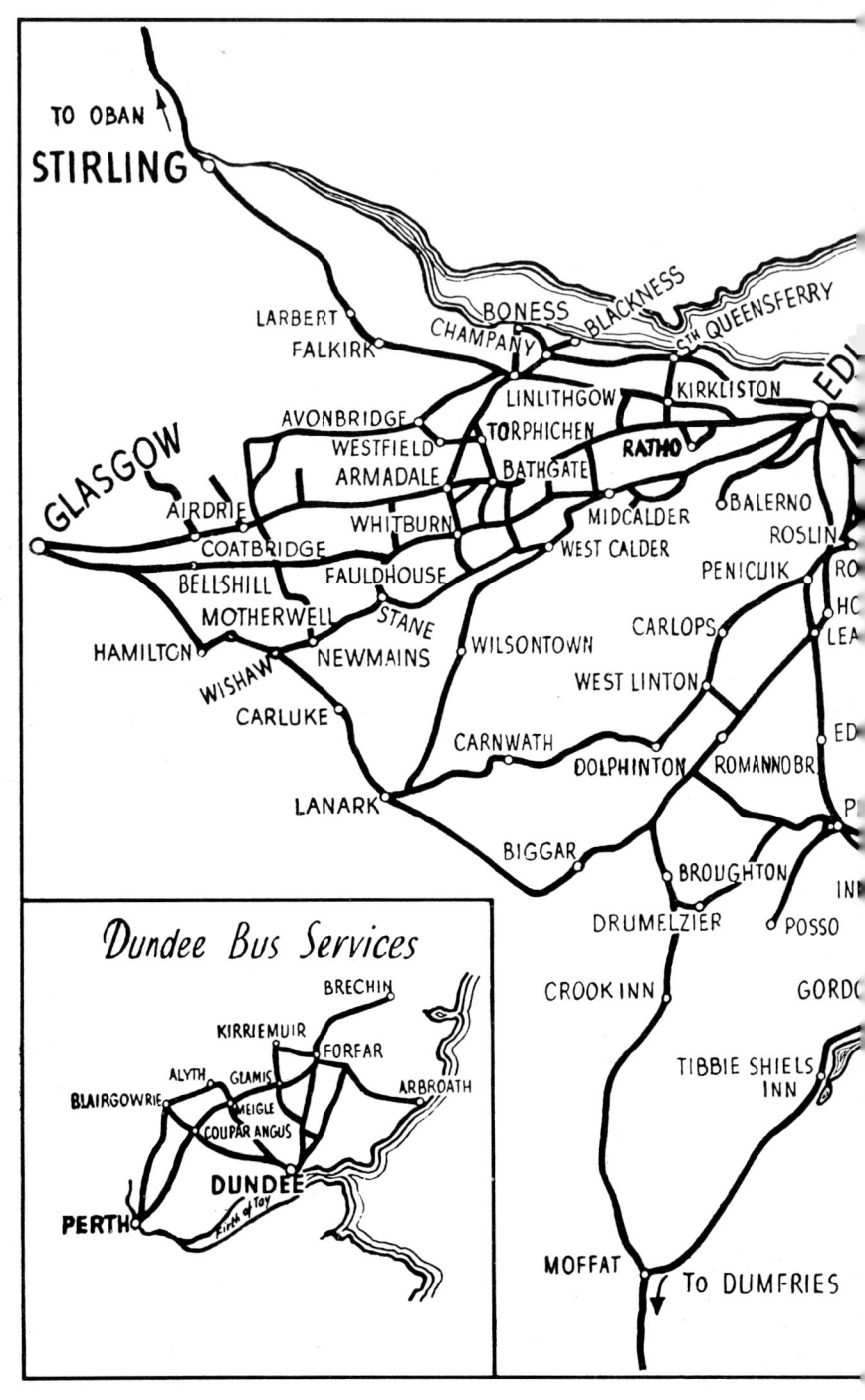

31. New buses in 1932 were A.E.C. "Regals" with 34-seat bodies by W. Alexander. Their petrol engines were later replaced by oil engines and after the war they received new 35-seat bodies of the then current pattern. This is B65.

32. A.E.C. "Regal" coaches with 28-seat Burlingham bodies incorporating a toilet compartment were introduced in 1933, and similar 32-seaters without toilets in 1934. One of the former type is shown, B70.

33. The first Bedfords, in 1933, had 20-seat Burlingham bodies as C14 shown here, though they had been preceded in 1930 by a few Chevrolets with 14-seat coach bodies by Alexander Motors, Edinburgh.

34. A Leyland Tiger bus of 1933 with 34-seat body by Metropolitan-Cammel, H101. Some had Burlingham bodies similar to those on the 1934 A.E.C. Regals shown in the next illustration.

35. A.E.C. Regal bus of 1934 with 34-seat Burlingham body, B104.

36. A Bedford 12-seat coach, S.M.T. body, of 1934, C30.

37. A front entrance was adopted for the 1935 A.E.C. "Regal buses" with 32-seat bodies by W. Alexander. This one is B142.

38. The Leyland "Tiger" buses of 1935 with 34-seat Cowieson bodies retained the rear entrance and introduced the flared skirt. H108 is shown.

39. A few Duple-bodied Bedfords added in 1935 also had rear entrances and were painted a very dark blue. This is C44.

40. Bedford coaches of 1936 with 20-seat Duple bodies were also in the very dark blue style. C57 is shown.

41. Six Leyland TS7's with 22-seat full-front Burlingham bodies incorporating a toilet compartment were supplied for the London service in 1936. They also were painted very dark blue and carried names on the back. H141 "Lady of the Lake" is the one shown.

42. There were also sixty Leyland "Cheetahs" with 36-seat full-front rear entrance bus bodies by W. Alexander in 1936. This one is T34.

43. The 1937 Leyland "Tiger" buses had 35-seat bodies by W. Alexander. This one is H174.

44. The coaches also had bodies by W. Alexander and seated 35. They were in a cream livery with red trim for the Coronation. This one is H186.

45. Another eight coaches for long distance services had 30-seat Duple bodies. Note the small crown on the door of H199.

46. Fifteen Leyland "Cheetahs", with 35-seat W. Alexander bodies in the cream livery, arrived in 1938. T61 shown here was the first of them.

47. There were more A.E.C. "Regal" buses in 1938 with 34-seat rear entrance W. Alexander bodies of which B182 is the example shown.

48. Also in 1938 there was a further lot of Leyland "Titan" double-deckers. This one is J48.

49. The A.E.C. "Regals" of 1939 had front entrance 35-seat bodies by W. Alexander painted in the cream livery. Those 1940 seated 39 and were also in the cream livery, but on them the trim was blue; B198 shown here is one of the 1939 lot.

50. The Leyland "Tiger" buses of 1939 were very similar to those of 1937, but the 1940 lot had the same bodies and livery as the A.E.C.'s of that year. The one shown, H255, is in the 1949 green livery with horizontal trim as then applied to some buses.

51. The first A.E.C. double-decker, one of two allocated to S.M.T. in 1942. BB1.

52. S6, a Dennis, also supplied in 1942.

53. Several Guy double-deckers were also supplied in 1943-5 with utility bodies by various builders, most of them originally painted grey. E18 shown had a Weyman body.

54. Double-deck utility bodies were provided for some pre-war Leyland "Tigers" in 1945. This is J72, formerly H112.

55. The first post-war additions to the fleet in 1946 and 1947 were A.E.C. "Regals" with 35-seat bodies in cream livery. The 1946 bodies were by Duple, the 1947 ones by W. Alexander. B295, one of the latter, is shown.

56. Many more arrived in 1948 with W. Alexander bodies and also some with Burlingham bodies in blue livery. Many pre-war A.E.C. "Regals" were rebodied with these W. Alexander bodies and some with similar bodies by Croft, as well as the Burlingham ones. B28 is shown rebodied with one of the latter.

57. Bedfords with S.M.T.-built 29-seat bodies were also added in 1947-8. This is C181.

58. The forerunner of the Burlingham "Seagull" pattern coach body arrived in 1949, on A.E.C. B364, here shown with improved front styling.

59. Burlingham also provided more orthodox 35-seat coach bodies for more new A.E.C.'s in 1949. The one shown is B370.

60. Several pre-war Leyland "Tigers" were rebodied with these too, such as H56 shown.

61. A.E.C. 53-seat double-deckers were also bought in 1948, 1949 and 1950, with bodies by W. Alexander, Duple and Burlingham respectively. BB87 is one of the Burlingham lot.

62. The A.E.C. Mk IV underfloor engine coach appeared in 1951 with 30-seat body by W. Alexander incorporating toilet compartment. The 1952 lot lacked this and seated 40 instead. B441 is one of the 1951 lot.

63. More of the 30-seaters with toilet and a different styling came in 1953. This one is B478.

64. The Burlingham Seagull pattern coach body with 30 seats was provided for more new Bedfords in 1952, while some earlier post-war Bedfords received 24-seat versions of this body. Many earlier A.E.C. "Regals" were also rebodied with 35- or 37-seat Burlingham Seagull coach bodies. This is a Bedford 30-seater, C191.

65. Fifteen A.E.C. "Regals" of 1948 were also rebuilt with full-front bodies. B340 is one of these.

66. The first Bristols arrived in 1954 — 38-seat coaches. A629, the one shown, is of a later lot.

67. D1, one of five Guys rebuilt with 39-seat S.M.T. bodies.

68. S1 was an experimental lightweight 32-seater built by the company themselves in 1955.

69. A large number of A.E.C. "Monocoaches" was bought in 1954-7. This is B429 of 1954.

70. A.E.C. "Reliances" with 41-seat Park Royal bodies followed in 1956. B543 is shown.

71. Double-deckers of 1956 and 1957 were 60-seat Bristol "Lodekkas". This is AA620 of 1957.

72. There were also some Leyland PD2/20 double-deckers in 1957 of which HH548 is shown. (Travel Press & Publicity Co. Ltd.)